EXAM SKILLS

Kate Brookes

Illustrated by Jennifer Graham

a

Text copyright 2002 © Kate Brookes
Illustrations copyright 2002 © Jennifer Graham
Published by Hodder Children's Books 2002
This edition published in 2005

Editor: Isabel Thurston
Design by Fiona Webb

10 9 8 7 6 5 4 3

ISBN-13: 978 0 340 88396 9

Printed by Bookmarque Ltd, Croydon, Surrey

The paper and board used in this paperback by Hodder Children's
Books are natural recyclable products made from wood grown in
sustainable forests. The manufacturing processes conform to the
environmental regulations of the country of origin.

Hodder Children's Books
a division of Hachette
338 Euston Road
London NW1 3B

Contents

Introduction

If given a totally free choice between revising and exams, or a few months lazing on a beach, you'd no doubt start looking for your beach towel and sun-cream. Why swot when you can swim?

Once upon a happy time, exams were a thing of school, college and higher education. With today's very altered job market, rapidly changing technology, emphasis on qualifications and opportunities for re-training, your skills and knowledge may continue to be assessed throughout your working life. The sooner you discover how to be a revision and exam wise guy, the more time you'll be able to spend on the beach.

Each chapter of Exam Skills takes you bit-by-bit through the test and exam routine. In Chapter 1, cold water is thrown on some fearful exam myths. Chapter 2 is about a very important person (not telling, find out for yourself), and Chapter 3 is about thinking like an examiner. The best and smartest revision plans, tips and techniques will be found in Chapters 4, 5 and 6. With revision done, Chapters 7 and 8 turn to the exams – how to organise yourself in the last days and hours, and what to do when the invigilator says "You may start".

I want to thank those past and current exam entrants who shared their tips, whispered their worries and made me laugh. The names and quotes have been muddled to avoid embarrassment. Huge thanks also to all those helpful teachers, who didn't run away when they saw me walking towards them, notebook in hand.

Success is so within your reach.

Kate Brookes

CHAPTER ONE

Exams – fact and fiction

"I made myself ill because I was so anxious revising for exams. I got the whole thing totally out of proportion and my marks suffered. I'm working towards AS-levels now and my approach is much more sane. I don't think about them as exams, just as routine tests done in a different room."

Genna (17)

"Don't worry too much about exams. All you have to do is have a go and do your best. There's more to life than school results. Compassion and self-respect are priceless."

Dean (17)

The e-word – fiction

Mention revision, exams, tests or assessments and everyone, especially those not sitting them, will let out a groan. The dreaded e-word can set up a nervous twitch among friends, teachers, parents and even distant relations. Let's get real, let's separate myths from reality and put exams in perspective.

Once the mythical beasts have been slain, the path is clear for you to tackle revision and exams with an attitude that is heaps more positive.

Myth 1: Surprise!

"Exams sort of creep up on you. They're like monsters in a scary film – you know they're lurking, but they scare you stupid when they appear."

Max (15)

There's no surprise element in having tests or exams. They're part and parcel of the school year like the end-of-term concert, the annual egg-and-spoon race and volunteering to be library monitor. Ever since you munched your way through your first packed lunch, tests of one sort or another have been on the timetable.

Myth 2: Don't know what to expect

"You never know what to expect in any exam."

Dirk (15)

You and your classmates have sat more spot quizzes, recap tests, assessments, mocks, modular tests and exams than any other generation. Most of you, for example, will be sitting your fourth or fifth national test since starting school. (At an equivalent stage in your parents' education, they had most probably never sat a national exam!) Because you have been through the test routine so many times there is little if anything that could shock. You know only too well what is expected – that you creatively regurgitate the stuff you've studied in class and apply it to imaginatively phrased questions. Rest easy because you can expect more of the same in the next tests or exams.

Myth 3: It's make or break time

"I know that these exams are not the be-all and end-all, but everyone makes out they are."

Eric (15)

Any sort of test, national or otherwise, is another stage in a learning-assessment process that started in playschool, rolled on through infant, junior and senior school and may continue into your working life when you choose or are required to upgrade your knowledge and skills. The essential thing to take on board is that exams of any kind are a measure; it is what *you* gain from learning that is important.

Exams are stepping stones, not the mountains that many make them out to be, and how you approach moving from one stepping stone to the next is up to you.

Myth 4: You must panic

"Exams have become mega competitive. Kids want to do better than their friends, and schools want to out-do other schools. No wonder everyone gets so stressed."

Jessica-Mae (15)

"Teachers and parents act as though normal life stops when revision starts. I was feeling really positive until they came over all worried."

Russell (16)

Sadly, there is some truth in what Jessica-Mae and Russell said. A major panic can be communicated from anxious teachers and parents. It is equally true that kids raise the temperature of exam fever. They start to feel under pressure, pick up on the exam frenzy put about on TV and radio and in magazines and newspapers and soon you've got a spiralling cycle of exam stress. But all this panic stems from no good cause — people somehow feel that exams deserve getting worked up about. You, on the other hand, know that exams require a totally calm, cool and collected you. Panic? No way!

Myth 5: Examiners want to trick you

"Exams are just too scary to even think about."

Judy (13)

Scary rumours that exams are loaded with trick questions and that exam setters are nasty and exam markers even nastier, are just myths. The fact is that if you know what an exam expects of you and what the exam marker is looking for, then suddenly the eeeek!!! goes out of exams.

You and your teachers have been working together to prepare you for exams that are *suited* to your level of ability. Preparing papers that suit candidates without undermining confidence is a keystone principle of the examining boards.

Here's another important thing to remember – exam markers desperately want to give you marks every time your paper shows evidence of relevant knowledge, understanding and skill. They definitely do not rub their hands in glee if they find a mistake.

There are definitely no gleeful sniggers at exam board headquarters if an embarrassing mistake or insoluble question appears in an exam paper and causes you and thousands of other kids upset, grief and lost time during an exam. Exam boards and everyone else in the testing business also go bright red should an exam paper be circulated before the exam. Whatever the mishap at HQ, your exam result will not be compromised. If in any doubt, the school will request a re-mark or tackle the issue, whatever it might be.

Myth 6: It is the end of life as you knew it

"Exams are crucial because they determine what you will and won't be able to do in the rest of your life."

Melody (16)

"No matter what sort of student you are, exams overtake your life."

Sashira (15)

There is a lot of pressure for you to believe that exams are 'make or break', but they aren't the be-all and end-all they are often made out to be. There is life before and after exams, and if you play your revision cards right there's life during exams. It is pure fiction that to do well in exams you have to lock yourself away in a study dungeon, deprive yourself of human company and revise night and day for months and months on end.

Myth 7: Exams are a joke

"Exams – total joke!"

Alex (13)

"They're just a way of making sure us kids do some work."

Alicia (15)

"No one can tell what you're capable of from a 90-minute exam."

Melody (16)

Academics have been arguing about the merits of exams since forever. Despite all the worthy discussion, no one has come up with a 'better' plan than the current one used in schools – assessment based on a combination of coursework and exam performance. (Not so long ago, results were based only on exam performance.) This combination aims to provide a more level playing field for all types of students – coursework allows those who do not perform at their best under exam conditions to shine, and vice versa.

Good news – the facts

With those soul-destroying myths revealed to be pure fiction, here are the important truths that will encourage you to glide through revision, and win in tests and exams.

There is a lot in it for you

"I only sat for my Year 11 exams because I had no choice. As far as I was concerned they were not going to help me become a better athlete. Anyway, I tried my hardest and I did okay. That's when I realised that exams are about challenging yourself even when the going's hard."

Pete (17)

"All that effort for a piece of paper is what I thought about exams. But that piece of paper, my coursework folders and my charm helped swing a place for me on an art and design course."

Trevor (16)

No matter how you feel about that 'piece of paper', everyone who sits an exam should be dead chuffed. Revising requires determination and a whole heap of self-discipline, while squaring up to an exam paper brings all sorts of inner strengths to the surface. There will be moments during the whole revision and exam thing when you'll surprise yourself – you'll master stuff you thought beyond you, plan an essay you know is a winner, and be more organised and in control than ever before. All powerful stuff for boosting self-esteem.

On the practical side, tests and exams will help you and your teachers determine your best options for further study, and give you an opportunity to spot which subjects spark your interest and could become major players in your future plans.

Coursework and exam results also tell a future employer, training college or academic institution that you can work under your own steam and use time well, you are motivated and organised, brimming with skills, and can do all manner of sorting, reasoning, research and presentation.

Time is on your side

No matter how much or how little time you set aside for revision, it is going to help. There are revision jobs that can take as little as five minutes. Be kind to yourself, though, by starting in plenty of time so you can revise bit by bit.

Easier than expected

Though few say it as they leave the exam room (exam papers are usually described as diabolical), most students find exam papers easier than expected or at about the level they expected. There are heaps of reasons to explain why you expect a proper drilling in an exam, but the main one is because you suspect those who set the exam questions. Remember, exam setters can only ask questions based on the curriculum syllabus. (In other words, they can't dream up any old question just for fun.) That's the same syllabus you have covered repeatedly in class, in revision and in previous tests.

It's an attitude thing

"I went through the exams last year and I'm still here and still smiling!"

Ian (16)

Once you accept that revision is not a form of medieval torture, that exam markers are not out to get you and that all students will be treated fairly, it should help you muster some positive attitude.

Remember, you've got loads to gain from doing the exams. This, more than anything else, is crucial. Feel upbeat and you'll be in the right mood for tackling even your least favourite topic.

The gang's all there

The thing about revision and exams is that you and your friends are in it together. Put your heads together so that revision timetables allow you to chill out together, study in groups, swap notes, ask for help, test each other or simply gossip for a while. But it's not just your friends who are there for you. Teachers understand only too well, as do family and neighbours, and friends who have done exams. If you ever start to get that 'I'm all alone' feeling, make sure you talk to someone.

Less than you think

You only have to revise the material you don't know. This may seem obvious, but you'd be surprised how many kids feel they should revise and revise again, absolutely everything. Cut the job down to size by working out what you do and don't know.

Are you primed and ready? It's time to find the perfect revision strategy to suit your personality and style.

CHAPTER TWO

Know yourself

Here's something that's not news – everyone is different. But what *is* news is that revision (and therefore tests and exams) can be a lot easier and more successful if how you do it suits your personality, your way of learning and your lifestyle. So before you set to planning a revision timetable (Chapter 4) and choosing revision techniques (Chapter 5), it's time to get to know yourself a little better.

Read through the following and tick which of the quotes under each heading describes you best. Then, highlight or jot down the tips that will help you design a revision package that fits you like a glove.

Rock around the body clock

 "It takes me so long to get going in the morning it's almost afternoon!"

Russell (16)

 "Mornings are my best time without a doubt."

Boos (15)

Morning people, full of beans first thing, should revise early in the day, perhaps even doing the hardest bits of revision first to take full advantage of their buzzing grey cells. Unwind and set yourself up for quality sleep with exercise and socialising in the afternoon or early evening.

Those who are in drowsy pyjama-mode until lunchtime can draw up a revision timetable for afternoons and early evenings. But to avoid the temptation of an all-day lie-in, schedule in some fresh air, exercise and catching up with friends in the morning. This will ready you for afternoon revision and guarantee that you don't feel life is one endless session of work.

TOP TIP

Working with your natural body clock means that you'll be revising when you're most effective and positive.

Powers of concentration

"Five minutes after starting to revise a topic, I'm thinking about the next thing I'm going to do. Help!"

Leslie (15)

"I start out fine, then my attention and eyes start to wander and suddenly the pattern on the carpet is the most interesting thing in the world."

Joss (14)

Concentration is all about being able to focus on one chosen thing (not the carpet!) for a *chosen* length of time. That you possess the power to concentrate is certain, but bringing it into play is sometimes the problem. This is usually caused by being unsure or fuzzy about *what* you're doing, *why* you're doing it, *how* you're going to tackle it and for *how* long, *where* you're doing it, and *what* the rewards are for completing it.

These aims, goals and rewards need to be written down, because once in black-and-white they will help you focus and therefore concentrate. When you feel your attention wandering, look at your aims, goals and rewards to bring you back on track. (See also *So boring*, opposite.)

"Once I get into a topic I can't stop until it's completed. Then, I'm too tired to do anything else."

Shaun (15)

This is the reverse problem – you become totally immersed for too long, causing concentration burn-out. It's great to be so focused, but is information being properly absorbed, understood and sorted? The brain, like a muscle, gets tired and can only cope with so much information. Instead of marathon revision sessions, try lots of shorter sprints with less ambitious goals.

> **TOP TIP**
>
> *Stick to your chosen time limits (shorter revision periods are better than long ones) and take breaks. Running over your time limit could lessen your sparkle for the next topic on your revision plan.*

So boring

"I start full of enthusiasm, but it doesn't last."

Jat (16)

"I can't sit still for more than 10 minutes. Not a lot of help when I'm trying to revise."

Emma (16)

B oredom and concentration wipe-out go hand-in-hand.

You can prevent boredom by shortening the revision period and taking a break, or by jiggling your revision plan to get a more inspiring mix of topics.

The most effective move, though, is to spice up your whole revision act by pick 'n' mixing every study method in the book (See Chapter 5) and by livening up what you're revising with cartoons, illustrations, pictures, spider diagrams and graphs. The simple introduction of coloured paper and pens can also ignite your interest.

In addition, revamp your study area so that it is somewhere you want to be. It can even help to have on hand a bottle of juice or water and a few healthy nibbles. If you're a born wanderer, select a couple of places where you can study comfortably without interruption.

Keep the feel-good factor going with rewards for work well done.

TOP TIP

It is easy to talk yourself into being bored. Boring is a word that slips so easily off the tongue. Often it is not boredom you're feeling, but tiredness, frustration or anger. If you're feeling down, spend a couple of minutes sussing the real reason and finding a real solution.

L for learner

We all learn in different ways depending on which senses are the strongest. The more you can use dominant sensory powers – sight (visual), hearing (auditory) or touch (kinesthetic) – the slicker your revision.

Read these quotes, see which best describes your sensory hot spot and then use the tips to help you revise on the fast track.

> "When I try to remember something it comes back as pictures, sometimes even moving pictures."
>
> Ginny (14)

This indicates a strong visual memory, so convert notes into diagrams and pictures for storage and snappy retrieval. You may well be able to recall information during an exam by dragging the image of a page of notes from your memory and 'reading' it.

> "I can hear a song once and remember the words. Can I use this to help me revise?"
>
> Warren (15)

Warren has an auditory hot spot, which means that if he hears something a number of times he will remember it (though once won't be enough). During revision, the auditory learner should record their own revision tapes and play them back, or take in educational programmes offered on CD-ROM, the internet, TV and radio.

"I'm great at hands-on subjects, but I glaze over when I'm faced with a page of text."

Lottie (14)

Feedback for the kinesthetic learner (who relies on touch) is strongest when the revision involves moving some muscle. Handwriting, for example, provides muscular feedback so you will up your retention every time you refine and improve your revision notes. You also benefit from getting out of your chair and acting out a topic using lots of movement and gesture and by turning straight text into a practical activity.

TOP TIP

While one sense may be more developed, you shouldn't ignore the others. Even your sense of smell can be an aid to memory. To exercise your sensory powers, check out Chapter 5.

Team-up

"I work better with someone else. Left alone, I just fiddle about and get nothing done."

Nick (16)

"I've tried studying in the library but all I do is people-watch. I get more done when I'm by myself."

Alison (14)

"I need to talk things over. It helps me get my ideas straight."

Kath (14)

One of the most common revision moans relates to feeling cut off from normal life and friends. The thing is, revision doesn't mean locking yourself away. Sure, there are times when zero distractions and total quiet will help you focus on a knotty topic, but equally there's plenty to be gained from teaming-up with a friend. All you have to work out is when you (and your mate) will benefit from sharing study space and when you need to go solo. (See also page 67.)

If you're easily distracted, then your biggest problem may not be friends but your family. A family going about normal activities can create a lot of din and disturbance even when they are making a big effort not to. Other than taking advantage of the silence when you're home alone and stressing to your family that you need peace and quiet, you can help yourself by finding alternative places to study. An elderly relative's house may provide quiet, for example.

TOP TIP

Even though sticking to your normal routine and having a settled study space is important, you should try anything and everything in order to make revision really effective.

Study zone

"I've got five younger brothers and sisters so to escape the racket I used to study in my mum's car which was parked on the driveway. It was really cosy."

Dominique (16)

"My dad goes ballistic, but I really can study while listening to music."

Sam (14)

"One thing I do know is that I can't work when my room is a tip."

Niall (16)

Only you know what it takes to make your perfect study zone. For some it's a neat desk in a quiet corner; for others it's a relaxed, messy space. Music – especially favourites that you know by heart – can help you study by camouflaging regular household din, blocking the sound of the TV in the next room and the hum of traffic outside. Where you do your revision isn't nearly as important as doing it.

There is a saying that goes like this: "The brain can only retain what the bottom can sustain." In other words, look for a study zone that is comfortable and has good lighting and ventilation (not too hot or too cold). Also make sure it is somewhere that inspires you. If your post-exam reward is a special holiday, stick up a photo of your destination to remind you of why you're working so hard.

TOP TIP

At some point while revising it is a good idea to do tests or past papers in exam conditions. That is, at a clear desk, in silence and without distractions. Even better if you complete the paper in the prescribed time.

Mood swings

"I will do anything – even tidy my room – instead of studying."

Jeremy (15)

"There are days when I really get into revision. Then there are those days when I seem to be wasting my time."

McKenzie (14)

Your downer on revision (and the exams) could be caused by lacking a personal goal. Motivate yourself by writing down what you want to achieve in the exams and what a particular result could mean for your future plans. In other words, decide what's in it for you!

Once you've nailed down some goals and feel positive about them, set yourself an easy topic and stick at it for just 20 minutes. Then, close your books and do something else: do some exercise, phone a friend or even tidy your room (if you're in the mood, of course). Later, do another 20 minutes and pile on more rewards. You'll soon discover that revision in small doses isn't too awful. Gradually increase the number of 20-minute study periods you do each day.

Keeping yourself in the mood is about keeping your interest up and this is best done by using every study trick in the book (see Chapter 5). If there comes a day when you simply can't open a book, don't fight it, do something different – see a friend, go to the cinema, swim 50 laps, go skateboarding. Nothing is surer to kill your enthusiasm than studying when nothing is being achieved.

TOP TIP

Starting your revision as early as possible will mean that you can take time off when you're simply not in the mood. Leaving revision to the last minute gives you no escape route. Sorry.

Have you got a plan?

"I've always kept my school diary up to date. If I didn't I'd never know what I had to do and when."

Jack (16)

"Planning is something I don't do. It's just not in my genes."

Edward (13)

If you're already in the habit of organising your time using a diary or planner, you'll have no trouble creating a revision timetable that suits you. If it is something you've not done, you could be making revision harder than it has to be.

A revision plan doesn't have to be a complicated, minute-by-minute thing. All it has to show is what subjects or topics need to be revised, how much time they'll need and when is the best time for you to revise them.

The most important element in the whole scheme is deciding what you need to revise. Don't waste time and energy revising a topic that you really do know.

Time bandit

"I can blow a whole hour fiddling about, clearing my desk, finding the right pen and raiding the fridge before I've opened a book."

Serena (14)

"I can stick to a timetable, but sometimes give myself too much to do."

Warren (16)

If getting started is the problem give yourself a set time to start revising each day and stick to it. Any desk tidying and fridge raiding must be done before the start time. Equally crucial is to take short breaks and finish studying at a set time.

To make sure the time bandit doesn't run off with precious minutes during a revision session, write down what you are going to get done and tick off each goal as it is achieved.

It is always best to have modest goals for each revision session. Use the leftover minutes to quiz yourself, master spellings and definitions, smarten up revision notes or memorise important dates or facts. Don't cut a revision session short – use it to the fullest.

When your goals regularly exceed the time you allowed, go back to your timetable and schedule in a couple of extra sessions for that particular topic. Do the re-jig of the timetable immediately so that it doesn't cause you any worry at all.

TOP TIP

Your revision timetable is not set in concrete – you created it, therefore you can alter it. You may need to change it because you're working faster or slower than expected, have realised you work better at different times or want to get a better mix of subjects.

Under pressure

"I freeze as soon as there is any pressure on me. Deadlines are my worst enemy."

Clive (15)

"If I have to get something done by a certain time, I do it no matter what it takes."

Laura (16)

Pressure can be a good thing – it can spur you to meet a deadline, score a certain grade or master a tough topic. But too much can be crippling, meaning that the pressure is so great that instead of boosting your efforts, you feel unable to do anything. Too little pressure and you may leave revision until the last minute. Being motivated by just the right amount for you is a tricky thing to predict.

A well thought out revision timetable should allow you to pace yourself. You should be able to maintain a steady working rate broken by short breaks and longer chill-out times. Always remember that you've got to have piles of energy in reserve for the actual exams. The revision period should be a gentle warm-up.

Here is a guaranteed way to avoid feeling under pressure. Start revising as early as possible and decide what you need to revise. Break down each topic to be revised into small units and then slot these into your tailor-made revision timetable (see Chapter 4). Stick to your timetable and cross off each completed task to prove to yourself that you are in control and staying well on top of your targets.

TOP TIP

If you start to feel negative pressure and can't suss a reason, talk it over with someone in the family, a friend or a teacher. A form tutor who is familiar with you and your work and what is required for each exam will quickly spot a flaw in your revision plan or the methods you're using for revision.

Everyone is an agony aunt

"Everyone gives me revision advice. How do I know what will work?"

Diane (13)

Around exam time there is an avalanche of revision tips and exam advice. You'll find tips on the web and TV, in magazines and in newspapers, and even ancient Aunt Agatha has a few top maths tips tucked up her cardie sleeve. Listening to these gems of wisdom won't hurt, but you have to decide if the advice is helpful to you. A successful revision plan is the one that suits the way you learn and work. You – not Aunt Agatha – have to be in control!

Do it for yourself

"My friends are going to pull great results out of the hat."

Lucy (14)

"I know I'm going to let everyone down."

Russell (16)

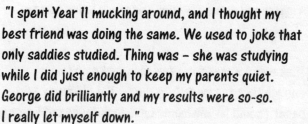

"I spent Year 11 mucking around, and I thought my best friend was doing the same. We used to joke that only saddies studied. Thing was – she was studying while I did just enough to keep my parents quiet. George did brilliantly and my results were so-so. I really let myself down."

Amy (17)

The only way to keep yourself confident and buoyed through revision and exams is to know you are doing them for yourself. Don't live up or down to others' expectations and don't compare yourself to others. Work out your own goals and stick to them.

CHAPTER THREE

Examining the examiner

"I kept putting off doing past test papers because I was frightened I would find out how much I didn't know."

Seerah (14)

"Because I was ill for a few months I didn't have enough time to revise fully. Instead, I did every test paper I could lay my hands on. I soon found out which topics I had to study."

Ben G (16)

If you were meeting someone for the first time, natural curiosity would drive you to find out about him or her – appearance, likes and dislikes. That you should be equally curious about the nitty-gritty of your exams is not only natural, but also cunning.

When training a football team, the manager sizes up his team's abilities and compares them with the skills of other teams in the league. For each game, the manager will devise new strategies and alter the line-up so that his team has the advantage. Knowing the plays and line-up of your exam papers gives you the advantage.

Keyword – familiarity

The keyword for this chapter is familiarity – it is your goal-stealing advantage. By the time the invigilators utter those dreaded words "You may start," you should be so familiar with the format of the paper and how it is put together that only the questions themselves will be a surprise.

Even then the questions won't be a real surprise because examiners don't want it that way. The aim of an exam paper is to provide a way of measuring teaching and your learning, and to give you guidance on future studies and career choices. Nothing would be gained from giving you questions on topics you have never been taught.

A good exam paper:

- is directly related to and reflects the syllabus you have been taught, learned and then studied
- is suited to the level or tier of ability for which you have been prepared
- does not undermine your confidence
- is fair in all respects, as is the marking.

Like it or not, exams produce qualifications and if you want to get on, you have to have qualifications.

"I am going to work with horses and I want to do more than just muck-out. A good result in this exam will give me the qualifications to go on to do stable management, maybe as an apprentice, and courses in leisure and tourism or business studies."

Brooke (16)

Gaining confidence

"If you look at the stacks of work you've done, revising is a job for 'Mission Impossible'. But when you look at the exam papers, it doesn't look half so scary."

William (15)

Knowing what you can expect and what is expected of you will boost your confidence during revision and in the exam. You'll be certain of revising the right material and confident that once in the exam, you can apply yourself to the job of answering the right questions in the right way within time limits.

REVISION

PAST EXAM PAPERS

"In class we analysed exam papers as examples of non-literary text. We looked at things like language and meaning, clarity of instructions, format and presentation. I gave the science paper 7 out of 10."

Twinks (14)

"I really got into doing old exam papers. Sad maybe – but really useful."

Mike (16)

So what do you have to know?

Head separate pieces of paper with the name of each exam and its date, time, duration and location. If a subject exam consists of two or more papers, you'll need a piece of paper for each, and don't forget to include language orals, modular tests or practical assessments, for example.

For exams at 16, also include details of which examining board administers each subject exam and which specification you have been entered for. (Your school has these details, if they haven't already been supplied to you with the timetable, rules and requirements, and statement of entry.)

Work your way through the questions opposite, writing the information under clear headings. Keep these notes somewhere handy so that you can add to them. You are bound to gain more insight into each exam as you revise and pick up tips from friends, teachers and revision books.

"When I get stressed, my head spins and I get in a muddle. That's why I spent time doing old papers. I was still a bit stressed in the exam, but I didn't get into a muddle because I knew what I had to do."

Laverne (17)

"Things look worse when you don't have all the facts. Like they say – knowledge is power."

Libby (16)

1 What topics will be covered? (What is the syllabus?)

2 What types of question formats are used? (Essay, short answer or multiple choice, for example.)

3 What is the total number of questions on each paper and how many marks are allocated to each? Once you have this information, you can work out how much time to allot to each question. Use this when doing practice questions under exam conditions (time limits, specified equipment only and no help) and as a guide for the actual exam.

4 Are there compulsory or optional questions?

5 Do the questions become more difficult as you progress through the paper?

6 Do you write your answers in the question booklet or in a separate booklet?

7 Are you allowed to scribble notes (for example, an essay plan) on the paper? If not, where?

8 What equipment do you need?

9 Does assessment or coursework contribute to the final mark? If so, how much?

Where to get the low-down

Curriculum and syllabus information (to answer question 1) will come from your teachers and school. If you want to research it further, the school may have copies or you can read all about it on the web (see pages 122-3).

As soon as the test and exam season starts, shelves everywhere groan under the weight of copies of past and sample papers. If your teachers don't bury you under copies of past papers, check out the school library. There may be limit on the borrowing period on some titles and others may be for reference only. You can also download sample papers off the web, though check that the source is reputable and that the paper is based on a recognised syllabus. Revision guides also have sample papers.

Poring over past papers and dissecting them will give you the answers to questions 2 to 7.

For question 8, you need the official equipment list. This comes from the examining board via your school. Make sure you get a copy and keep it safe.

Subject teachers are your best source for question 9. If you're not 100% sure, check.

What does the examiner expect from you?

The three magic words are – knowledge, understanding and skill. In various ways and usually at the same time, your answers will require knowledge, understanding and skill.

Knowledge: what you know and can recall.
Understanding: what you can explain.
Skill: what you can do and how well.

Equally important is that your answer is appropriate and relevant. For it to be both these things, the answer must show that you have understood the question, and have answered it in the requested manner using knowledge, information and skills that actually relate to the topic. A magnificent piece on the Suffragettes will score nothing if the question was 'What contributed to the outbreak of World War One?'

How to get along with exam markers

"I know I am doing these exams for me, but I also know that I have to deliver what the examiner wants."

Tamara (16)

"There's no point getting angry with the test paper. It won't change anything."

Bobby (15)

"When answering a question, think like the exam marker."

Andrew (17)

1 Do precisely what the examiner wants. No doubt about it, he or she likes to get his or her own way. An 'I'll show you' attitude won't get you anywhere.

2 Listen to the invigilator. The instructions and guidance they give you come direct from the exam boards.

3 Follow instructions provided on the paper – they are clues that direct you to giving the answer the marker wants.

4 Say what you mean! Exam markers are not mind readers and they can't give marks for something that is in your head, but not on the page.

5 Make your writing legible and your presentation clear. It makes it so much easier for the marker to see every mark you have earned.

6 Use terminology that is relevant to the subject and show that you know the meaning.

7 Check your work. Exam markers get upset when silly mistakes, such as spelling or punctuation errors, cost you marks.

8 Give full answers to get full marks. Sometimes the addition of just one or two specific words makes the difference between half and full marks.

9 Show your working out.

10 Don't write the question on the paper. Exam markers know the question only too well and they don't want you wasting valuable time.

"I'm dead scared of exams. I know I'll fall to pieces on the day."

Jeremy (14)

Above all, exam setters and exam markers want you to be able to do your best. They don't want you to panic, freeze-up or fall-apart. They know you do your best work when you're relaxed. For more exam room hints and tips, see Chapters 7 and 8.

CHAPTER FOUR

Revision – ready, steady...

"I left revising until the last minute and I will never do that again. The worry is not worth it. I'm no genius (just ask my mates), but it's got to be better to start early."

Steven (17)

It doesn't matter what you're revising for – a national test, a music exam or the theory part of the driving test – knuckling down and sorting your revision plan is time well spent. A well thought through plan makes the difference between cool cruising and crisis cramming.

Ready for a night out?

"When my brother did his GCSEs I joked about his multi-coloured study timetable. Now that it's my turn to revise, I've decided that a timetable is nothing to laugh about."

Leanne (15)

Think of your revision strategy like this – exams are like a night out, and your revision plan is getting everything you need together so that you look your best and feel your most confident. Getting ready for a night out may involve deciding on a look, finding the right clothes, having a relaxing soak in the bath, and ages in front of a mirror. If you know what needs doing and get it sorted, then you'll have a great night.

What night out?

Do no planning and leave everything to the last minute and you're bound to find that your favourite jeans are in the wash, everything else is lying crumpled in your wardrobe, there's a queue for the bath and no time just to get ready. That's one date (or your exams) washed out because you didn't do the necessary planning way back. That's the difference between crisis cramming and keeping cool.

It's an individual thing

Even for a night out, everyone has different things they've got to do and different ways of doing it. If you know, for example, that you need an hour to get dressed and another hour deciding if you look okay, you leave enough time. It's the same with your revision plan – it should take into account all aspects of your personality, behaviour, strengths and weaknesses, good and bad habits, and lifestyle.

Did you know?

Here are just 10 reasons (there are heaps of others) for devising your own revision plan. It will ...

1 take into account when you are at your best and most alert.

2 revolve around must-do commitments.

3 fit in with deadlines for on-going school work.

4 put you in control; and knowing that you are in the driving seat is very empowering.

5 give you plenty of time off to relax and get some exercise.

6 let you schedule in extra time to get to grips with difficult topics.

7 allow you to put maximum effort into those subjects that are crucial for your future plans.

8 save time because you won't be wondering what you should be revising this morning, this afternoon, tomorrow, or whenever.

9 let you work at your own pace and use revision methods that suit you.

And last, but not least:

10 A good revision plan that is followed will give you the confidence to shine in the exams and maximise your results.

Hey, but I'm spontaneous

"I've never revised for any sort of test and I always do okay."

Alec (13)

There are times when spur of the moment stuff is perfect. Because you've winged it without a minute's revision through module or recap tests doesn't necessarily mean you can breeze through nine or more exams over five weeks and answer questions on work you did in class 18 months before. You and your brain are a great team, but it isn't fair to expect so much of this partnership over the long period of the exams.

When should you get down to planning?

"I started revising for my mocks a month before. Until then I was loaded down with coursework. It wasn't ideal. If you have time, give yourself three months."

Sedge (17)

"I wouldn't advise anyone to begin revising less than eight weeks before exams. I gave myself a month and worked extremely hard with no time off. Not a good idea, as my results showed."

Bonnie (16)

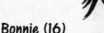

Start planning your revision as early as possible. The more time you give yourself, the better. If you have an evening or weekend job it would be a good idea to start cutting down on your hours if you can. Start revising in a laid-back way five or so months before the exams. Or work at a steadier pace three or four months prior. (This revision may cover you for mocks, trials and module tests, for example.) Three months before the exams, teachers will be reminding you that revision should be underway. Eight weeks before, their tone will have become sterner. The average period of revision is about eight weeks.

"People say exams aren't that important, but they change their tune if you say you aren't going to bother to study."

Eddy (14)

To encourage revision at this time, teachers will go over topics, give recap tests, dish out loads of useful advice, hand out past papers, and urge you to speak up if there is anything – to do with a topic, exam requirements, timetables, rules or equipment – you're not clear about. Teachers are not saying this to fill in class time – they really do want to help you.

What does a revision plan look like?

"My best friend's study plan is really detailed and almost covers a wall. Mine is really simple and because it's smaller it looks a lot less frightening."

Briony (14)

"I based my revision timetable on an Advent calendar.
I could open windows to reveal a reward for working
so hard. Bit childish, but it worked."

Tristan (16)

"My plan for revision is really ordinary. I write down
topics to be done each day in my school diary."

James (13)

There are as many ways of drawing up a revision
plan as there are students sitting exams. Some will
look like a countdown for a rocket launch – highly
detailed with every minute accounted for; others
will be more general. What it looks like just isn't
important, though it helps if it is colourful and dead
easy to follow.

What you need

- A diary, desk calendar or wall calendar (make sure
  there is plenty of space for you to write in) or a
  large sheet of paper which you can rule up to make
  a calendar. If you're into spreadsheets you can, of
  course, create a timetable on screen.
- Paper, writing stuff, eraser and ruler. It is a good
  idea to write up your plan first in pencil so that you
  can make changes along the way.
- Fancy stationery – stickers, for example – and
  coloured pens to highlight important bits.
- School timetable, homework diary and exam
  timetable (or at least start and finish dates).

- Text books, subject folders and perhaps your most recent tests and reports.
- Any advice from your school, teachers, curriculum authority or examining boards.

How to do it

Now that you're geared up you can start to plot your revision plan following five easy steps.

"I used different colours for each subject and stickers to mark exam days."

Steve (16)

Step 1

Fill in: exam details; deadlines for projects, coursework and tests; regular must-do commitments and special occasions; holidays and study leave.

Step 2

Head separate pieces of paper with each exam and jot down topics that you know need special attention. A topic might deserve special attention because it is crucial for your future plans, because it is worth a lot of marks or because it is an area of weakness.

If you've never felt confident about symmetry, or congruence, now's the time to confess. This list covers the topics you don't know and you will give these topics more of your time. Under the heading 'Do know', list topics which need only light revision.

Don't fall into the trap of thinking that every single topic deserves mammoth revision. It is simply not the case. There are always topics that you find much easier to understand than others. A quick look at class tests, homework or assignments will soon prove that point.

Using text books, subject folders and every scrap of curriculum and exam advice to hand, make sure you've not missed out any topics or listed a topic under the wrong heading. If unsure, show your 'don't know/do know' lists to your teachers.

By now your room will be a tip – books everywhere – but the hardest and most brain-sapping stage is over. Time to take a fresh-air break.

TOP TIP

The better your grades or levels in the core subjects – English, maths, science – the greater the career options. Even if one or more of these subjects is not your favourite, it's worth devoting adequate time to them in your revision plan. You'll be grateful for it when you eventually start to apply for jobs.

Step 3

Decide when you do your best work. It could be very early in the morning and for an hour or two in the afternoon. You might be useless before noon, so choose to study in the afternoon or evening. In pencil, mark on your planner when during each day you're going to study, avoiding any clashes with commitments or other deadlines and allowing plenty of time to relax and get some exercise.

How many hours you turn over to revision each day depends on how early you start before the exams, what you want to achieve, your attitude and energy, and how you work. If you're unsure of what will work for you, just plan the first week of your revision then assess if it was successful.

"It's not the amount of revision that matters, it's the quality. If like me you feel pushed for time, it's important to make the work you do meaningful."

Sedge (17)

No doubt you've heard the saying "It's quality, not quantity that counts", and it applies to revision. Five hours straight studying sounds impressive, but scientists know that concentration wavers after about 40 minutes. Studying for hours results in a bored you and a tired brain, so don't do it.

The best plan is to study for about 25 minutes, then have a 10-minute break away from your study zone. You may stick to the 25-10 routine for one, two or three hours each day – it really does depend on you. Start with two 25-10 sessions, see how you feel and how much you achieved and then slowly increase the number of sessions.

TOP TIP

The 25-10 routine is all about thinking and working in minutes. You'll be surprised at how much you can get done in as little as five minutes when you put your mind to it. Thinking in minutes also helps in exams when you allot 'x' minutes to each question and to checking over your paper. Measuring in minutes keeps you on the ball.

Step 4

Start to pencil topics into each of your 25-minute revision sessions. You can use your school timetable to pick the subjects (see pages 78-79), but try to muddle up the topics so that you get an interesting mix – an easy topic, a harder topic and a favourite topic. You can start with an easy topic to build your confidence, move on to the more taxing one and then reward yourself with a favourite topic. Some people like to get the hard stuff over with when they are fresh, and take confidence from knowing that the topics that follow will be easier or more enjoyable.

You can choose to do topics from one subject during a study period. For example – reading a scene from Shakespeare's 'Romeo and Juliet', studying the language of Shakespeare; and doing a sample essay on 'Romeo and Juliet'. Or, you can hop between subjects – English/non-fiction text, maths/handling data and science/chemical reactions.

"Do your least favourite subjects first, then the rest of the day can only get better."

Jessi (16)

Underestimate what you think you can achieve in a 25-minute session and how many sessions you can do in a day. It is better to feel fresh and positive after studying, than to push yourself too hard causing burn-out, frustration and dark clouds to follow you around.

TOP TIPS

- *Quiz time – allow time (10 to 15 minutes is usually plenty) for self-testing or for someone to quiz you. You can build this into your plan or do it whenever it suits.*

- *English and drama texts – a 25-minute session may not work well when you're reading to get a firm grasp of language, plot, character, setting, etc. In your plan, you might like to dedicate whole days to this. To keep focused, write notes or record your impressions as you read. Don't forget to take regular short breaks.*

- *Schedule in times when you can do past papers or full essays under test conditions and time limits.*

- *Don't burn the candle at both ends. If you study early in the morning, don't attempt to study again late at night. Try to stick to your normal routine. If you feel on top of the world only after nine hours sleep, this is not the time to catch just four hours kip a night.*

- *Varying the topics and subjects you do will help keep your interest up, but so will varying the revision methods you use. (See Chapter 5.)*

- *Try to include topics from every subject during a week of revision. Don't, for example, totally ignore a subject simply because it's your last exam.*

- *As a particular exam draws close, you will naturally want to do more revision on that subject. Don't let an imaginary panic take over and tempt you to a hard cramming session in the last two or three days.*

Step 5

After a week of using your plan, assess how it is going. If you can answer 'yes' to each of these questions, you have created the perfect plan.

1 Are you on top of your revision?

2 Are you scoring well when self-testing?

3 Are your revision notes shrinking?

4 Are you relaxed and feeling confident?

"Take breaks and go to bed early. Congratulate yourself on how much you know and how you really deserve a good rest."

Sedge (17)

"I spent a whole day getting my head straight about what I had to revise. When it was done and I knew what work I had to do, I felt so much more confident."

Deborah (15)

Your revision plan is there to help you. It should make you feel in control as you see, session by session, your revision load getting less and less.

It's a goal

"I know what I've got to do and I'm great at drawing up lists. Thing is - that's all I do - plan."

Charlie (14)

"I look as though I'm studying, but deep down I know I'm just mucking about."

A. (13)

To get you motivated and focused, write down your goals or targets, and the rewards. There may be big goals and rewards at the end of the exams – a chance to do your preferred options, a place in college or university, a job, the ultimate party, luxurious lie-ins, a holiday, etc.

Every time you start a revision session, you should also have a mini goal or tiny target. Jot down what you are going to achieve in each 25-minute slot. At the end of the session, check if you have done it.

A tiny target might be 'Learn 20 words of German travel vocab', 'Re-do algebra problems and score 100%' or 'Understand keyword notes on cell activity'.

Whenever you miss a target, you'll know immediately and can pencil in another revision session. That way you always feel in control.

TOP TIP

In the United States, research revealed that students who wrote down their long- and short-term goals were more successful than those who didn't.

"I wasted a lot of time checking up on what my friends had studied. If I hadn't studied the same stuff, I panicked that I was falling behind. It was so stupid."

Alexa (17)

CHAPTER FIVE

... Go!

This chapter is an Aladdin's Cave of hot techniques, vital skills and nifty tricks to make revision easier and a whole lot more interesting. Keeping yourself motivated and interested is half the battle and to do that you need a whole armoury of revision tools.

"Some techniques work for some people, not for others. I would advise anyone to make notes on the need-to-know issues."

Sarah (15)

Pick and choose methods that suit you, making sure you try those that use your dominant senses (see Chapter 2, page 17). If you have already used particular methods and found them successful, then continue using them.

"For history I write a basic summary of the period without referring to my books or notes. It's surprising to see just how much you do know."

Gavin (16)

How do you learn?

Learning and knowledge come from understanding. If you don't truly understand something, your knowledge and recall will always be a little fuzzy. The magic of understanding is that it is more efficient, and recall is much higher than with rote-learning or memorising. Once a topic is understood the brain makes connections between lots of relevant knowledge. Maybe it's best to imagine it as a superhighway full of hyperlinks.

To understand a topic:

1 Break it into small, easily-managed units.

2 Focus on the topic (brain switched on), use revision methods that best suit you and be an active reader.

3 Compile really good summaries in note form, on posters, or on tapes, and constantly question yourself to make sure you are understanding what you're studying.

4 Go over your notes, revisit web revision sites, replay tapes, practise exam papers, etc. to check your recall and depth of knowledge.

5 Be interested in what you're learning. With a little imagination even logic gates can be riveting. When motivation goes for a walk, think about your goals and rewards.

6 Give yourself time. Your ability to remember something decreases rapidly after 24 hours. To keep retention up, revise learned material regularly. The more times something is effectively revised, the better it is remembered.

Leonardo da Vinci, no slouch in the brain department, had a five point technique for sharpening his wits: ask questions all the time; develop all your senses – hearing, touch, sight, taste, smell – and use them as learning tools; read widely to gain general knowledge; learn to draw; and accept that everything is connected to everything else. If it worked for Leonardo, it's bound to work for you.

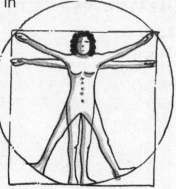

Acronyms

An acronym is about reducing a list of words to just one or two easily remembered words. The newly formed word is created by taking the first letter of each original word. It doesn't matter whether the acronym is a 'sensible' word as long as it is memorable. Here are some examples:

'Mrs Gren' is an acronym of the characteristics of living things – movement, reproduction, senses, growth, respiration, excretion, nutrition.

'Eatsme' is the levels in the atmosphere in order – Earth, Troposphere, Stratosphere, Mesosphere, Exosphere. To make sure you don't confuse Earth and Exosphere, the first two letters of 'Earth' have been used. Clever, huh!

Active reading

This is about reading with the brain totally switched on. Your starting point is setting a goal. (Diving into a book without knowing what you're looking for will guarantee interesting but useless diversions and time wasted.) Your purpose may be to gain information or a better understanding and to answer a question, harvest more facts, solve a problem.

The active reader keeps focused by taking concise notes in their own words or highlighting important information in the text itself. At the same time they are compiling a glossary of words and meanings, definitions or memory tricks (see *Get a catchphrase* and *The right word*, later in this chapter).

While reading you can also ask yourself questions about the text. What did that last sentence mean? What was the author trying to say? Is the language effective? Have I understood the issues? What is the meaning of that word? What were the causes and effects?

"When I can't understand something, I read it again holding a ruler under each line and I read out loud."
Wyre (14)

Active reading is done at a relatively slow speed, and because it requires lots of concentration and effort, go at it for only short periods. If you feel your attention lessening, take a short break and restart only after you've reminded yourself of your reading goals.

Develop your active reading as it will come in handy when reading exam instructions and questions.

Any questions?

It doesn't matter whether you are reading, revising your notes, studying with a friend or practising essay planning: always ask yourself questions. Regularly quizzing your knowledge, understanding and skills will immediately prove whether you're on the ball or dozing on the sidelines.

After reading a page of notes, say on the Chartists, ask yourself why the landed, upper class felt threatened by this movement.

A picture paints a thousand words

It is very inefficient (and not half boring) to attempt to understand, know and remember page after page of hand-written or typed notes.

If part or all can be turned into pictures, graphs, spider diagrams, pie charts, cartoons, timelines and flow charts, you'll not only up your understanding, knowledge and retention but the lively look of your notes will up your attention. You will also be happier about revisiting your notes.

Big is beautiful

Make billboard-type signs using snappy language and attractive images to help you learn important pieces of information. Don't try to put too much information on the poster – keep it simple. Mount the posters in prominent sites only – on the fridge door, on the back of the loo or front door, on your mirror or by your bed. Every time you look at the poster, read the information out loud and try to take a mental snapshot of the poster.

Chain gang

While you are revising and your brain is absorbing and storing information, you are also building chains of information. Sometimes the first link in the chain is just a few keywords, but when you see or recall these words it sets off a chain reaction and other links of information are recalled. In the exam, the chain reaction will be started by keywords in the questions.

You can help make the links in the chain by reducing information to a series of keywords or images and linking them (as in a spider diagram) to each other with lines and arrows.

When the chain reaction doesn't happen or isn't complete, it means that you don't fully understand the topic.

Get a catchphrase!

An alternative to a one- or two-word acronym (see page 55) is a phrase that is created using the first letters of a list of words. The catchphrase has to be easily remembered, so make it as weird and wonderful as you like.

Here's one to get you started – 'My Very Eager Maid Just Swept Up Nine Pins' is a catchphrase for the order of the planets in our solar system (Mercury, Venus, Earth, Mars, Jupiter, Saturn, Uranus, Neptune, Pluto).

In a flash

Buy some blank index cards or cut your own from a sheet of card and on one side write a keyword (see Keywords opposite). On the other side of the card, write down all the important information related to that keyword. Test yourself by picking a card at random or by asking someone to test you. Your target is to recall every bit of information on every card. When a keyword is mastered, separate it from the pack so you don't waste energy on something you already know.

Flash cards like these give you three revision opportunities – once when you are looking for information about the keyword, then when you are writing the flash card, and again during quizzing.

Look after yourself

Rest, relaxation and enjoying a healthy diet are vital revision tools. Not only do they set you up for revision and exams, but being fit and healthy makes you glow with positive attitude.

How do you eat an elephant?

Bit by bit, of course! Huge chunks of information can be hard to absorb, so break the information into smaller and smaller units. Tackle each unit one-by-one (if dealing with a complicated issue, sentence by sentence if necessary) and reward yourself at each stage.

Keywords

These are very important words and short phrases that sum up critical, must-know information. To make them leap off the page underline them, highlight them, surround them in stars, make them enormous or do them in a different colour.

As your revision progresses, you will be able to glance at a keyword and make links from it to the relevant information.

Knotty clues

Tying a knot in a handkerchief isn't at the sharp end of memory technology, but when seen or handled the knot will prompt the information.

A visual or tactile cue can even be taken into the exam room. A coloured thread tied around the top of a pen could remind you to use paragraphs more often. A friendship bracelet, tied around your wrist could prompt the formula for the circumference of a circle. Make three knots in the bracelet to represent the three elements in the formula – $2\pi r$.

Mnemonics

This is any sort of device that helps you remember. Acronyms are a mnemonic, as are number-letter codes, silly rhymes and catchphrases. Your teachers will know some of the best, and new ones keep popping up in revision websites.

For anything you find you cannot fix in your memory, try making a mnemonic of your own. It doesn't matter what it is as long as it works for you. You are guaranteed to remember it.

Mountains into molehills

"There's so much stuff to revise, I'll never get through it, so why even start?"

Nigel (14)

It's easy to understand why the whole notion of revising can be frightening. Your imagination goes into overdrive when you guess at the amount to be done. First thing to do is pack away the imagination and unpack the cool, collected you.

Secondly, stop guessing what has to be done and go through which topics you know and which you don't. Once that is done, the chances are you will have cut your revision in half. Then, divide those topics into ever smaller units. Once you know what has to be done, there is nothing to fear.

Finally, get down to it and start ticking off each unit as you do it.

Practice makes perfect

Revision is more than just filling your brain with loads of information that you can retrieve during the exam. It is also about learning how to use what you know. The best way to do this is to do past test and exam papers and practice papers. With every practice paper you do, you're becoming familiar with the format of the paper and how to allocate your time. You are also testing that your knowledge is complete and that you can retrieve and use the right pieces of knowledge, understanding and skill at the right time. Practice and more practice with real questions is especially important when it comes to perfecting essay planning and writing.

Though you should try to do old exams under exam conditions, you'll also benefit enormously by regularly attempting a few questions from past papers. Build time for this into your revision timetable.

Rhyme time

Nursery rhymes are unforgettable, so silly rhymes are another tool in your revision kit. Make up your own rhymes and don't worry if they don't scan like a Shakespeare couplet.

This rhyme fixes the date when poor Anne Boleyn got the chop:

In fifteen hundred and thirty six,
Anne Boleyn was in a fix.

Scanning

This is when your eyes move rapidly and logically over a paragraph or page of text looking for particular words, numbers or phrases. Scanning lets you race through pages of text – there's no time wasted reading something of no use – but for it to be of help in revision, swap to active reading when you spot a target word – a date, proper name or specific term.

If you can't specify target words, scan for capital letters (which will indicate places and names); numbers or symbols; bold, italic or underlined text; picture and diagram captions; and any text that is preceded by a bullet point (•), star (*), number (1, 2...) or letter (a, b...). Skimming the first sentence of each paragraph can also give the gist of what follows.

Use scanning when researching to fill gaps or check information in revision notes and when refreshing your memory of set texts that are generously littered with your highlighting and notes. You can use scanning for a final read-through of thoroughly revised notes. When you hit a keyword, stop and ask yourself 'What do I know about this?'

Secret code

This code can be used to turn a hard-to-remember date or string of numbers into picture words similar to Egyptian hieroglyphics.

The only hitch is memorising the code. You can create your own or use this rhyming one.

1 = bun   *2 = shoe*
3 = tree   *4 = door*
5 = hive   *6 = bricks*
7 = heaven   *8 = gate*
9 = wine   *10 = hen*

1945= bun wine door hive

Sound effect

Especially suited to the auditory learner, recording and listening to educational programmes is beneficial for anyone revising. If nothing else, it's a way of revising when you're out and about or want to lie in the sun.

Listening to ready-made material is fine and your teachers will be able to recommend the best. But for a real test of your understanding and knowledge research, script, produce and record your own. At every stage of production, you are bedding that topic into your brain.

Introduce music into your programme – simply 'hearing' the music in your head during the exam can be enough to open memory floodgates – and use voices, sound effects and changing volume to make certain pieces of information stand out and to keep your attention. When scripting, use different writing and presentation styles – the BBC journalist-on-the-spot, daytime TV dribble, teen agony, sloppy drama or stroppy soap.

Keep the recordings short – five to ten minutes is plenty. Better to record lots of short pieces than one long, boring one that you never have time to listen to.

Team mate

Like a good set of revision notes, a friend you team up with to study can be one excellent revision tool. You can keep each other motivated, do question and answer sessions, swap and mark essays, and share knowledge and understanding. You can have one revision mate or a whole network; you can work face-to-face, swap ideas and notes on the phone or by email.

For the group study thing to work, you have to hammer out some rules. The most important one being that gossip is reserved for break times. Agree to study the same topic for a set time, say 25 minutes, and after a 10-minute break, revise by quizzing each other for 10 minutes.

Talking to friends can help you to assess your progress, but it can also send you into an unnecessary flap! Don't forget that different people study in different ways and at varying speeds.

Sweet smell of success

Our sense of smell is very powerful and the slightest whiff of something familiar will spark memories. Aromatherapists – those who work in the scent business – say that certain scents can even aid memory. They suggest sniffing peppermint or rosemary essential oil – a couple of drops applied to a tissue is plenty – every so often as you work.

The experts also suggest that your recall of a topic may be triggered if you take a tissue dabbed with the associated scent into the exam room. Just hope everybody else is not doing this!

Take note

"It's not reading notes that makes information stick, it's making them."

Sarah (17)

The most common starting point for revision is to create a set of revision notes. Writing starts the thinking process, helps you link ideas and encourages you to be organised and logical.

Revision notes should be written in your own words (no word-for-word copying from books), and the aim is to extract only the most important pieces of information and to summarise them using the fewest number of words. While doing this you are also checking whether you understand the information. If you don't understand you won't be able to express it in your own words, and your recall will be poor.

Within the notes, underline or highlight crucial words (called keywords) or facts, and translate some text into pictures, graphs, diagrams and flowcharts (see *A picture paints a thousand words*, page 57).

As your revision progresses you should keep trying to shrink your notes until you can fit each topic onto one or two sides of an A4 page or index card. As certain pieces of information become knowledge, they can be omitted from your notes or further summarised. Each time you re-do your revision notes you are actively learning and storing information. Don't discard old revision notes, you may need to refer to them.

"My writing starts neat but ends up a scribble. My mum suggested I use small writing for my revision notes. It worked – everything was legible."

Myfanwy (14)

Other features of good revision notes:

- They are easy to read and clear. If you hand write your notes, the muscular feedback can aid memory.
- They are colourful and keep your attention.
- Quotes are correct and sourced.
- Each set of topic notes or cards looks different. This will help visual recall.
- They save loads of time because you won't be rummaging through three year's worth of class notes to find something.
- They include lists itemised by bullet points, numbers or letters.
- Abbreviations are used and are consistent.
- Headings clearly signpost the information.
- Diagrams, graphs and illustrations break up the text.
- Important keywords are highlighted.

Tall tales

Create an off-the-wall story to help you remember the chronology (order) of a historical event or natural phenomenon. Fill your tall tales with celluloid or paperback heroes, friends and family...the more absurd the plot the easier it will be to remember.

The Merry Reviser Show

This is a great learning tool if you're an auditory learner (if you have high recall after hearing something). It is also a fun way to share revision with friends and to get away from note-taking.

Pick a topic – for example, *What are the characteristics of non-literary text?* – and then, with a chat show type panel of guests and an audience, discuss it and throw questions to each other. For a really lively session, why not take on Shakespeare and discuss a theme of a play such as murder, love, lust, honour or madness?

The right word

The English language is brimming with words that sound the same or look similar, but have very different meanings. One way to unmuddle these words is to invent a wacky phrase that highlights the correct meaning. A stalagmite grows upwards, so remember the phrase 'mites crawl up'. A stalactite, which hangs down from the roofs of caves, conjures up the phrase 'tights fall down'.

Wacky phrases can also unmuddle incorrect spellings. For example, there's a **lie** in be**lie**ve, or **Liam** is in par**liam**ent.

As soon as you discover words that confuse you, create a wacky phrase and write it down, and highlight it in your revision notes.

Trouble shooter

"When I started revising I put huge question marks against things I didn't understand. I wish I had sorted them at the time rather than leaving them to the last minute."

Sanjee (16)

If you get stuck on a topic and you've put in a huge effort to understand it, you have to make a decision on what is the best strategy for you. No matter which you choose, don't get into a panic.

You can call it quits for the moment, close the books and tackle it using a different method in a day or two when you're refreshed. Don't leave it any longer than this – you may forget about it altogether.

Look for help from a teacher or friend, or you may find a piece of winning advice in a revision guide for that subject.

If you think that not cracking it will cause you more worry, then get stuck in. Break the topic into even smaller units – sentence-by-sentence, number-by-number – and go at it for short periods. To counter any negative vibes bring out some flash new stationery, start a clean sheet or find somewhere different to work.

Smile!

Improve your attitude and exercise some facial muscles by smiling! Even if you're not feeling particularly cheery after a session of revision, look at yourself in the mirror and grin. Remind yourself of successes and triumphs and of how much closer you are to achieving your goals and rewards... especially your rewards!

CHAPTER SIX

Help is at hand

"There are times when I feel like throwing every
book and revision note out of the window."

Guy (15)

No matter how much effort you put into starting
revision early and sticking to a plan, there will be
moments when it all gets too much. It may be just
one stubborn algebra problem that pushes you over
the edge. To make certain that one moment – one
microsecond – of panic and frustration doesn't turn
into an all-day, all-week downer, ask for help.

Asking for help isn't a sign that you're not coping.
Instead, it's a strong indicator that you are in control.
You've hit a snag, you know exactly what to do.
Agonising in stroppy silence – don't go there!

"I'm in the middle of my revision, feel totally lost
and no one understands."

Rebecca (16)

There's only one hitch when looking for help – picking from the very long list of willing volunteers! You really are spoiled for choice, whether you need to brain drain someone about 3D solids or find a shoulder to cry on.

"I want to thank Joanna for just being there when I was doing my exams. I would be all ready to rant and scream and throw things around the room and she would crack a joke."

Jon (16)

Teacher! Teacher!

At revision and exam time, your teachers are there for you in the biggest possible way. They've been on your side since your first day at school, though there may have been occasions when you doubted it.

"I'd been revising really hard and when I bottomed on a test, I just lost it in class and burst into tears. I looked at my teacher and realised she was upset, too."

Dawn (15)

Your teachers have been preparing you thoroughly for this stage in your education. All that nagging about keeping your homework diary up to date, planning your time and prioritising was groundwork for planning for your revision.

And all that emphasis on presentation – keeping books neat, ruling margins, underlining and making your notes attractive – was a warm-up for revision notes that are a joy to behold.

Those recap and module tests were not simply sneaky ways to measure if you had been paying attention and working, it was practice. Assessing your work and progress were rehearsals for the 'don't know/do know' stage in your revision planning.

"My school record isn't great, and I felt two-faced when I asked my maths teacher for extra help. I expected a lecture, but all she said was 'When?'"

Toby (14)

These hidden extras, which mean you have the necessary skills to create a revision plan and see it through, are, of course, woven into the teacher's mission of delivering the correct curriculum in the most memorable ways possible.

During the lead up to tests and exams, teachers will turn up a little revision pressure with spot quizzes, recaps and, of course, mocks. These tests are like the minor league races attended by athletes in preparation for a big race. They keep the athlete in just the right frame of mind and level of fitness so that they peak for the big race, which in your case are national tests and examinations.

One thing you don't do with a marked test or assignment during this period is bin it or lose it somewhere in your locker. Tests are not an end in themselves; you and your teacher can use them to spot any weak areas that need extra work. When a weak link is spotted, don't sit back and wait for the teacher to call you out. You make the first move and organise a time when the teacher can go over it with you.

> *"For years, my teachers have been saying 'This is the sort of question that will appear in your test papers'."*
> Mel (16)

Here are some other ways to make sure you get what you need from your teachers and your school.

- Stay after school or give up a lunchtime and join remedial, homework or subject study groups. During this stage of the school year, staff running the groups will let the students' needs dictate what is revised.
- If you and others in your form share the same problem, get together and ask the teacher if he or she can give you extra coaching. You will all benefit and your teacher will appreciate going over it once rather than 10 times.
- Do a test question from one of the hundreds of revision guides you'll find in bookshops. (You may also find copies in your school library.) Complete the test and ask the subject teacher to mark it.
- Present a copy of your 'don't know/do know' topics to each subject teacher and ask them to check if you've missed anything.
- Politely check with your teachers that every piece of curriculum and exam information has been passed your way. It's important that you are confident you know exactly what is going on.

"One thing I learned from my last exam is to check out rumours with someone in authority. This rumour was about a dead-cert question in the paper, so I studied this topic a lot and the rest only a little. The question and that topic didn't appear in the exam."

Kevin (17)

• Rumour, gossip and speculation abound before exams. Check out anything you hear with a teacher.

Make the school timetable your best friend

When your mind has turned to revising and your focus is seeing off the exams (and possibly waving farewell to your school uniform), school can seem a waste of time. You know what you've got to do and you just want to get on with it.

"Roll on study vacation! Studying AND keeping up with
school work is killing. What's a real waste of time is
PE. Since when has running around the playing field in
the rain been an examinable subject?"

Alexandra (16)

The best way to avoid any clash and to really benefit
from the school timetable is to go with the flow rather
than rampage against it. Moulding your revision
loosely around your timetable will mean that you will:

- be prepared for surprise quizzes
- have set aside time to revise for scheduled tests
- have planned in time for homework
- have a chance to look over a subject the night
  before and note down any questions or queries you
  want to raise in class the next day
- be able to revise notes taken that day while they
  are still fresh in your mind.

This is how you can make it work. Choose a few
subjects from Monday's timetable and pencil in those
subjects for revision on Sunday. For Monday
evening revision, pencil in a subject from Monday's
timetable and a couple from Tuesday. Keep going
through the rest of the timetable in the same way –
picking subjects to revise in advance and subjects
where you can revise what you covered in class that
day. (For more information on planning revision, see
Chapter 2.)

Choose the subjects for 'day before' and 'day of'
revision by being aware of each subject teacher's
normal routine. A teacher who usually sets homework

weekly and schedules tests on Mondays, for example, will continue to do so. Some teachers are also happy to let you know what the programme of work will be for the next few weeks.

Do a revision plan based on the school timetable for one week and try it out. If something hasn't worked, amend your plan. You can plot your timetable for weeks in advance, or continue doing it weekly.

Asking teachers for help is not a matter of clicking your fingers. Teachers cannot drop what they are doing the moment you realise your understanding of forces is shaky. Teachers, too, have timetables to follow and deadlines to meet. Getting extra help from a teacher requires organising, so the sooner you get your name on his or her list, the better.

Phone a friend

"A boy in my class was always phoning me with questions. In the beginning it was okay, but when he started to panic, I started to worry."

Joe (14)

"While I was studying, exams were all pain for no gain. But I'm proud of how I coped and how my friends supported each other."

Allyson (16)

Friends and family can be called upon at a moment's notice and you can rely on them to be a sounding board and much more. But before ringing a friend, especially one who is also studying, or giving a parent an earache, spend five minutes jotting down in point form what's worrying you. When it's straight in your mind, spend a couple of minutes looking for a way through it. If no solution appears, then get dialling and talking. The aim of talking about something that is bugging you is to find a positive solution, not to alarm a friend or deepen your own anxiety.

"Our tutor encouraged us to form study groups where we could help each other. He said that kids hold back from suggesting it because they don't want it to look as though they're sponging off their classmates."

Emily (14)

The ultimate sounding board for revision hassles and emotional ups and downs is a team of classmates who each have strengths in different areas. Your team may consist of a maths wizard, a language natural, an IT genius, and one who can be relied on for sound advice and a cool head.

"My best mates and I used to meet every couple of days during study vacation for a moan and groan session. After we each had a grumble, we would swap the best revision tips we'd picked up."

Ashleigh (17)

Been there, done it

A friend or relative who has recently taken the tests and exams you are sitting, is worth their weight in gold. They are evidence that there is life after exams! Tap them for revision advice they wish they'd known before their tests or exams.

"My cousin is a year behind me at school. When his exams came up, I was flattered that he asked my advice."

Amanda (17)

The home front

"I go off the idea of studying as soon as my mum says 'Shouldn't you be revising?'"

Rob (14)

R evision and exam time can be stressful for your family. They know that a happy and calm home environment is important, and they will want to achieve this. You can help yourself and your family by letting them know what is important to you. Here are a few tips to share with your family:

- Reassure them that if you need help, you will ask for it.
- You know what you're doing and are in control of your revision.
- You want support and encouragement, not nagging.
- You want them to respect your goals for these tests and exams.
- They must trust that you will do your best to achieve your goals.
- Rest, relaxation and exercise are crucial elements in effective revision.
- You will keep them informed about how you're doing.

"I don't think my dad trusts me to prepare for my tests. As soon as he gets home from work, he's on my back."
Samantha (14)

Each family is different and there may be special circumstances that could affect your ability to study at home. These circumstances could have a long history or crop up suddenly. In either situation, don't bottle up your worries or try to work in impossible conditions. As soon as you become aware of a difficulty, explain it calmly to your family and try to find a solution. It might be best to work at a relative's house or to use the library after school.

You can also turn to a trusted teacher, the school nurse, student counsellor, education welfare officer or head of careers information for help. Free-phone services, such as ChildLine, are also manned by staff who can offer advice (see page 123).

Whatever the problem, don't try to handle it by yourself. It is estimated that about one-quarter of exam sitters are trying to cope with a non-academic problem – bereavement, illness, family separation, for example. You're not alone and help is there for the asking.

Quick fix

Need a change or some different sources of information? Then simply push a button and log on to any one of the homework, revision and exam sites on the net.

Get recommendations from your teachers and friends, and look out for sites created by teachers from your area. Is the information on the school's web page? It might also be signposted on the local education authority website. The websites listed on page 122 have useful links.

Creating any sort of list of these sites would fill not just one but two books. Try all of the obvious search words – revision, exams, homework – and then narrow the field by naming the exam, test or level and the subject. Once in, the index and links will take you anywhere you want. Mark your favourite sites or record the web address; it saves a lot of time and gives you a chance to use the site to the fullest.

You'll also find addresses and descriptions for revision sites in teen magazines and in the education and kids' sections of newspapers. Not all are devoted to getting you knowledged up. Many are concerned with attitude- and confidence-building, health and diet, and coping with stress.

Help at the push of a button can also be had from TV. Once the revision and exam season starts, you'll find special time zones dedicated to revision topics. Unless your best time for working is in the small hours, you'll need to record these programmes for playback later. Details aplenty in any TV guide.

Because they don't want anyone to miss out, publishers and broadcasters produce their revision material in multiple formats. So if you have no internet access look for book, CD or video versions.

Being kind to yourself

Don't under-estimate what rest and relaxation, a good diet, loads of fresh air and a generous portion of pampering can do to your revision and exam performance. A physically fit heart pumps 20% more oxygen to your brain, and as oxygen is brain fuel it makes sense to keep fit and healthy.

The moment you let ill-health or tiredness through the door, negative attitude, lower performance and stress will be hot on its heels. The only way to keep these undesirables at bay is to be kind to yourself. It is an indisputable fact that everything is easier if you are happy and healthy!

Are you positive?

"This sounds corny but on the wall above my desk there's a poster that says 'You can do it!' I believe it and know that I can."

Sophia (16)

Being topped up with positive attitude sets off a chain reaction in the same way as keywords launch an information chain. The positive attitude flow chart goes like this...

Why not copy this flow chart and put it up in your study zone?

TOP TIP

Check your body language! Slouching over your work screams negative attitude. Pick up your attitude by sitting straight.

Take a break

"I hate studying like you won't believe. But when I feel myself getting tense and angry, I go to the park and sit on a swing."

Frankie (15)

Your revision plan is your first line of defence. Check it to make sure you're getting enough mini-breaks between revision sessions and enough time to relax and do other stuff. The aim is to feel in great form from the moment you wake up until the moment you go to bed. The first signs that all is not well are impatience and anger (usually directed towards yourself) over the silliest things, and tossing and turning at night.

TOP TIPS

- *Work out a dance or exercise routine to a piece of music that never fails to lift your spirits and inspire you. Run through the dance routine during a break.*

- *Don't go straight from studying to bed. Wind down gently with a book, a light snack or some gentle exercises. Be wary of TV – it can wind you up rather than chill you out.*

Go the wholesome way

"When I study, I get bored and then I eat. Exams are bad enough without looking like the Michelin Man."

Lynn (16)

Take in lots of good, wholesome food: fruit and vegetables, powerful proteins (meat, fish, eggs, beans, peas, nuts and pulses), wholegrain bread and cereals, rice, pasta and dairy produce.

Resist the temptation to munch on comfort food for a quick boost. Chips, crisps, chocolate and biscuits, are all known as junk food, for good reason. They are high in carbohydrates, sugars and fats, and while they may make you feel energised for a short period, you will soon be left feeling tired and bloated.

Without causing your body to go into shock, replace sugary, fizzy drinks and caffeine with good old water, pure fruit juice and herbal teas.

TOP TIPS

- *Eat little and often throughout the day.*

- *Don't even contemplate dieting. A balanced diet is the perfect diet.*

- *It's a bad idea to skip breakfast. Do so at your peril.*

- *Keep healthy nibbles and a glass of water on your desk.*

Fit to succeed

This is not just about walking, running or kicking a football about, it's also about making sure that your study zone is full of fresh air. There's nothing surer than stale air to set off a yawn.

The air in the average bedroom can be replaced by opening the window for 40 minutes a day, and the average yawn can be stifled by sticking your head out of the window and taking ten deep breaths.

TOP TIP

*Give over five minutes of a mini-break to power walking, jogging on the spot and stretching exercises. By exam time you'll be both clever **and** fit.*

Pamper the inner (and outer) you

"My big reward for lots of hard work was to get a haircut and highlights. You've no idea how much I looked forward to that day."

Tish (16)

Revising is hard work even when you've taken the easiest route, so lash out on some luxuries and pamper yourself. Put flowers on your desk, ask for your favourite meal, have an exam-free gossip, rent a video or DVD, or have a long bubbly soak in the bath. During this extraordinary time of revision and exams, it is often the ordinary things you hanker after.

TOP TIP

Get together with a friend and share some quality time doing something you both enjoy – watch a football match or go shopping. Plan it and do it.

Stress release

If you follow the advice on the previous couple of pages, you're seriously reducing any likelihood that the stress beast will get the better of you. Stress left to run amok prevents you from working, full stop, and it can affect you emotionally and physically. (See also Chapter 8.)

The symptoms of stress:

- Inability to go to sleep quickly and to sleep soundly.
- Feeling cut off from family and close friends.
- Low sense of self-worth and lack of confidence.
- A 'don't care' attitude.
- Breaking into tears or a rage for no obvious reason.
- Poor concentration leading to impatience.
- Loss of appetite.
- Regular or constant tightness in your chest that makes breathing difficult.
- Stomach tied in knots.
- Total lack of get up and go.

TOP TIP

Take the pressure off yourself by remembering that you are doing the revision and exams for yourself and no-one else, and that you will do your best.

"I'll try my hardest. That's all I can do."

Liesel (14)

CHAPTER SEVEN

How to gain marks

You're fully briefed on revision planning and techniques that can be used across all subjects. This chapter gets up close and personal with exam technique – how to gain marks, not lose them.

Some tips relate to specific subjects, especially English, maths and science, while others apply more generally to tackling questions in all subjects.

Look before you leap

"When you hit a question where you know the answer, don't start writing immediately. Read the question again. You may have missed a key instruction."

Jennifer (17)

Read the whole paper to get a feel for how it develops. As you read instructions, underline the important words – 'Answer *two* of the following questions'. Tick or circle questions you *must* do (compulsory questions) and your choice of questions you want to attempt (optional questions).

As you start a question or section in the paper, go back and double-check the instructions to make sure you're doing the right thing. Better to spend five seconds checking than five minutes answering the wrong question.

Marking time

From the total exam time, give yourself time to read through the paper and five to ten minutes to check it over at the end. The remaining time should be divided by the number of questions on the paper.

When allocating time, be guided by the amount of marks awarded for each question. A question worth 25% of the total marks deserves 25% of the time.

Hunt for clues

Questions contain useful information. They will certainly direct you to the type of answer expected, but they will also contain keywords to help prompt your memory. Don't take the question at face value, ask what it tells you.

If you find yourself lost for a word, spelling or idea, and memory tricks yield nothing (see *Memory Prompts*, page 104) then flick through the exam paper. You never know, you might just find the word you want or a link that dislodges the information stored in your brain.

Get it down...now

As soon as the exam starts, write down must-not-be-forgotten facts – a date, name, quote, chemical formula, a mnemonic – somewhere on your paper. Once they're on paper, you can quit panicking about forgetting them and focus on the exam.

Magic spelling

Exam markers can deduct up to five per cent from your marks for incorrect spelling. Ask someone in your family or a friend who's good at spelling to go over some of your class notes and assignments, spot the incorrect spellings and write a list of the correct ones. Learn and quiz yourself on 5 to 10 spellings a day.

Examiner knows nothing

Assume that the exam marker knows nothing about the subject. This means that your answer must contain sufficient, clearly expressed, relevant facts to bring the marker up to speed on the topic.

Don't skimp

Make sure your answers – especially short answer questions – contain all the relevant information. Full answers score full marks.

Crystal clear

Exams are not beauty contests, but if your answers are easy to read – legible and well-organised – it is easier for the marker to spot every mark you have earned. Clarity also applies to diagrams, labels and essay organisation. When labelling a diagram, graph or illustration, use straight lines with arrow heads to connect the label to the item. Don't try to fudge it – the examiner can spot a fudge a kilometre away.

Show it

Always show your working out! If your final answer is wrong, the examiner can check your working out to see if you understood the question and had the knowledge and skill to do it. If it shows any of these, then you may gain a proportion of the total marks.

Have a go!

Never leave a question unanswered. Clearly mark or note down questions unanswered and go back to them later. If you still don't know the answers, take educated guesses. Better to score one mark than none at all. In multiple choice, delete totally off-the-wall answers and choose an answer from those that remain.

Keep it short

In essay or in short-answer questions, keep your sentences snappy by sticking to the one fact per sentence rule. Keep your answers sharp and concise and your planning clear with one idea per paragraph. Both techniques will make your answers a breeze to mark.

Quality counts

Examiners are looking for quality answers, not long ones.

"French orals aren't that bad if you imagine you're talking to a French-speaking friend, not a teacher. Show off what you know, any fancy grammar constructions for example, but don't detour off the set topic."
Sarah B (17)

Quote, unquote

Collect a prize collection of short quotes, knowing the source (and, if relevant, when and where it was said) and show that you know the implications of the quote.

Know your source

To fully answer source-based questions that you will find in history exams, for example, you need to cover the following – who wrote it and when, reliability and audience, context or background, type of source, why was it written, and what was the effect. Read the source several times and underline keywords before preparing your answer.

Use the jargon

Even though a question may be phrased using everyday language, your answer should contain appropriate terminology. Water, for example, doesn't disappear when boiled, it evaporates.

Just do it

Do exactly what the question asks. If two lines are provided for an answer, don't write an essay. If you must place a cross in a box, do a *cross* – not a tick or smiley face – *in the box* – not next to it, below or above it!

What's the unit?

Lots of marks disappear down the plughole because the unit of measurement or the decimal point is omitted from the final answer.

Ooops!

If you have omitted an important bit of information, write the additional material at the end of your answer. In the main body of the text, neatly direct the examiner to the extra text. Better to do it this way than to use microdot writing squeezed into a tiny space.

Essay questions

From your first read-through of the question, work out the topic and theme. On the second, underline those words that tell you the style of your answer – e.g. a description or evaluation. Plan the essay and number the points in the order they should appear, then re-read the question to check that your plan adds up to a complete answer. If you are clear about the central point, your essay will be convincing and coherent. Five minutes planning is time well spent.

Are you checking out?

Leave 5 to 10 minutes to check your paper. Proof-read for spelling and punctuation mistakes, and errors in working out and factual information.

Key words

Make it your business to know exactly what these words mean. They are the keywords in most questions. Getting them right is crucial for exam smarts.

Account for: find reasons for

Analyse: break into parts and describe each part

Argue: present evidence and reasons to support or reject an issue

Assume: accept that the following is true

Calculate: work out the answer

Causes of: write about the actions or events that made an event occur

Comment on: explain why something is important and support your ideas with evidence or examples

Compare: describe how two things are alike and different

Contrast: describe how two things are different

Define: say what is the meaning

Describe: give a detailed account of;

Discuss: use argument, opinion and fact

Distinguish between: indicate the differences

Effect of: the results or consequences of an event

Estimate: provide an approximate answer, no need to work out exact value or solution

Evaluate: decide and explain how important something is

Explain: make plain

Explore: examine thoroughly from many viewpoints

Identify: clearly name all the relevant items or parts

Illustrate: use examples to explain something; do this using words – don't draw anything unless asked

Interpret: show the meaning
Narrate: tell the story
Outline: give the main features but not the details
Predict: suggest what might happen
Prove: use convincing evidence to show a statement is valid
Relate: show how things are connected
State: present in brief, clear form
Summarise: give a concise account of the main points
Trace: follow a development in chronological order
Write an account: tell the story

Core facts – English

"Our teacher said that the best way to revise non-literary texts was to read as many examples as possible and then discuss them."

Geoff (16)

Who's the audience?

Don't forget that a discussion on a non-literary text must include – Who is the intended audience? What is the writer's purpose? What is the main idea? Has the idea been developed and how? Is it coherent? How has the audience affected the writer's choice of language, structure, presentation and organisation? Has the writer succeeded in targeting the audience?

It's set

When answering questions on set texts, a complete response will cover characters, plot, setting, language and vocabulary, structure and style, purpose and intent, theme, and dramatic or important devices. Support your points with relevant quotes.

But ...

Exam markers have noted that students overuse the words 'but' (especially at the start of a sentence) and 'just'.

To divide or not to divide ...

There is some very creative word division going on in exam papers. Words that should remain separate are being joined – aswell, infact, alot. Equally common are no-no word breaks – some body, any way, with out, him self. These should be: as well, in fact, a lot, somebody, anyway, without, himself.

Punctuation

You will lose marks for not employing accurate use of language and syntax. Watch out for: capital letters to start a sentence, full stops to end a sentence, and the correct use of commas and possessive apostrophes. Brush up on these!

Get real

A piece of creative writing will come to life if you draw on personal experience. Writing about something you know will produce colourful vocabulary, a real sense of emotion, and lively facts and opinions. If you can make the examiner laugh or cry as they follow the twists and turns in your story, all the better.

Core facts — Maths

"The best way to revise for maths is to do past papers. They really give you insight."

Vik (15)

Formulae

Knowing formulae is crucial, but errors are caused by not knowing when to use them.

Golden oldies

Make sure you know by heart the relationship between fractions, decimals and percentages, and are confident with indices. For example, a number to the power of 1 (x^1) is itself, and any number to the power of 0 (x^0) is always 1.

Maths is one of those subjects that keeps going over old ground. So no matter how complicated the question appears at first, a bit of digging will unearth the common-or-garden maths beneath.

Make connections

Watch out for 'linked' questions, where information, a calculation or answer from the previous question should be used in the next question.

Factoring

After factoring, multiply out the answer to see if you get the original expression.

Very clever

Save time in maths multiple choice questions by mentally calculating what the last digit in the answer should be, for example: 334 x 412, the last digit will be 8 (from 4 x 2). Eliminate any answers that do not end in 8. Where an answer has to be expressed in certain units (kilometres per hour, for example), eliminate any answers without the correct unit.

Core facts — Science

"The thing about science is that it's almost impossible to bluff an answer. You either know it or you don't."

Declan (17)

Glossary

You have to a have a firm grasp of scientific terminology and meaning to get full marks on questions. If you haven't done so already, compile a glossary of terms and symbols and learn them.

Heavy metal

The properties of metals and non-metals and the characteristics of living things are exam favourites. Go that extra distance and memorise a mnemonic for each. The properties of metals, for example, comes out as SSHHEDDM: strong, sonorous, heat conduction, high melting point, electrical conduction, dense, ductile and malleable.

Photosynthesis ... again

A standard exam question, and for good reason – photosynthesis and respiration are key biological processes that you should know inside out.

Memory prompts

"Middle of my German exam and I went blank. That tiny little word I wanted was gone. I left a blank space and kept writing. About 10 minutes later, the word suddenly popped into my mind."

Michael T (14)

When a piece of information goes under cover in your brain, don't panic. Stay relaxed and use one or two of these memory prompts.

Forget about it

The harder you try to retrieve something from your memory, the further it can slip away. Call off the hunt and forget about it. With the pressure off, the stored information is more likely to come out of hiding.

It's on the tip of your tongue

This is a frustrating trick of the brain. You can almost visualise or hear the word or fact you want, but there's some annoying little bug in the system playing cat and mouse with it. Get around the bug by asking questions – It sounds like ...? It looks like ...? It starts with a ...? When did I learn it? It rhymes with ...?

Doodle

Write or draw anything on a spare piece of paper.
The process may open a memory channel that is not
activated by other prompts.

Where was I?

In your mind, go back to where you learned or revised
the information you are trying to remember. Once
back there, fill in as many other details as you can.
This mental walk will produce associations that may
help retrieve the memory.

Look!

Just look around the exam room – the walls, the
windows, the invigilator's choice of socks – when
you're trying to recall a fact. Simply taking your eyes
off the exam paper can be enough to prompt
a memory.

Who, what, when?

If you suspect an answer is incomplete, remember –
who, what, when, where, why and how. Ask questions
of your answer: do I have the who? Have I mentioned
what happened, when and where? Why did it happen?

"I can remember a couple of scary times in the exams.
Once, when I thought I'd answered the wrong question,
and then when I got confused about electrical circuits.
I panicked for a second, then said to myself 'You know
this stuff. Get it sorted.'"

Vince (18)

CHAPTER EIGHT

Let the exams begin ... please!

"If I see another set of revision notes, I'm going to scream. I'm totally fed-up with studying."

Shivali (15)

"I just want the exams to be over!"

Darcy (14)

Believe it, you are ready to close your books and sit the exams. Though few admit it, you and your mates can't wait for the whole show to just get on the road. You have had your fill of revision and test talk. Your brains are bursting with priceless knowledge, hard-earned understanding and stunning skills. All you want is for the exams to happen so that you can download everything onto paper, start to breathe easy and take your life off hold.

This chapter deals with what you should do just before the first exam, and how to stay on top throughout the exam period, no matter how tough the timetable.

"My revision timetable worked well. I knew what I had to do each day, but what do I do now that the exams have started?"

Stewart (15)

It's up to you

Any times suggested here are a guide. They are not carved in stone! You may feel you need more or less time in which to do final revision and to get physically and emotionally ready for an exam. The only one who can judge what is right for you is you. But be kind to yourself by allowing more time rather than less. Use any free time for chilling out.

"For a major swimming meeting, my coach adjusts my training so that I peak at the right time. I've paced my revision in the same way and now I just want the exams to start."

Ben (15)

Days to go

"My exams begin in three days and I feel like I'm at the top of a roller coaster – excited and terrified."

Justin (14)

When you first start revising, you divide your time between each subject. As the tests or exams draw closer, you focus more energy on those subjects that appear early in the timetable.

With three days until your first paper, it's time to zero in on the subject of the first exam and to be prepared for day one of the exams.

With just days to go, there are four things to do:

1 Revise ... again
2 Solve
3 Rehearse
4 Relax.

With only one subject on your mind, you can get an awful lot of quality re-revision done in three days. Stick to the routine you used during earlier revision, especially the 25-10 routine (see page 47) and periods of relaxation. As a rough guide, use one-third of your revision slots for final revision for the first exam; one-third for testing; and one-third for 'solve', 'rehearse' and 'relax' (see pages 114-121).

Revise ... again

"When the first exam was only days away, it was a massive relief to concentrate on just one subject."

Jodee (13)

"Revising everything for all subjects was like juggling eight balls. Revising one subject for the first exam made me feel in control again."

Phil (16)

It's time to clear your desk, walls and floor of everything except your notes for the first exam and, if you haven't done it already, to tape a copy of the exam timetable (with your exams highlighted) and equipment requirements somewhere prominent. The clear-up, along with all the suggestions that follow, is about giving you some breathing space in which to get things straight. In other words, to make sure you know you are in control.

Boxing clever

Though the 'out of sight, out of mind' principle is usually a good one, shoving revision notes for later exams under your bed is not really clearing up. Would you feel in control and relaxed knowing that you were sleeping on a time bomb of jumbled up exam stuff?

One nifty solution is to get cardboard boxes – you'll need one for each exam – and use them to store everything related to each exam. Label each box with subject name and exam date, and then stack the boxes where they won't distract you while you're revising for the next exam.

The best thing about exam boxes is that as each exam finishes, the number of boxes gets smaller. It is dead satisfying to take each box to its final resting place in the garage, the loft or the dustbin!

Know what you don't know

"I felt so good rattling off topics I knew inside out."

Sam (15)

To make the most of revision time and downtime in these final days, decide which topics deserve a major slice of your attention and those that require a memory-jogging read-through. Don't waste time or energy revising stuff that you know. Sure, read your notes and hit the keywords, but be conscious of the fact that this is 'known' material.

You can tell if you know something by the way a keyword will prompt you to recite out loud all the relevant information or for your brain to fill with associated images and words. There's only one thing to do with 'known' topics – slap a 'done' sticker on the notes and put them back in the subject box. As your revision-to-be-done shrinks, your confidence grows and grows.

Opposite are some super-efficient and effective ways of dealing with notes not bearing the 'done' sticker. It's up to you to choose which method best suits the topic and you.

- Re-write revision notes, but make them look radically different.
- Make a recording of your revision notes and then while playing them back, jot down keywords to make a spider diagram.
- Get someone to test you.
- Prepare essay plans using questions from past papers.
- Give yourself a few minutes to jot down all you know about a topic. You'll be pleasantly surprised! Promise.
- Check out a revision crib and make notes in your own words.
- Use memory tricks (see Chapter 5) to make hard-to-recall facts or concepts totally memorable.
- Ask for help – a friend may have found a snappy way of understanding something.

Testing times

"It's hard but doing real exam questions a day or so before the exam really gets your brain working."
Amber (15)

Knuckling down to answering exam-type questions requires real determination. The rewards, though, in terms of your results are more than worth it.

If you haven't done so before, get in plenty of practice allocating time to each question in line with the marks that can be earned. Then, do the questions within those time limits under exam conditions.

Vary the self-test diet by redoing class tests and assignments and by tackling questions on internet study sites, and in published revision guides.

To break the monotony of going it solo, get together with a friend and test each other. Do this by providing questions for each other and then marking them. That way, you'll learn from each other, discover any weak areas and you'll have a friend on hand to help sort any problems out.

Found a problem?

If you discover a topic that you cannot get on top of no matter how hard you work, don't get in a flap. Best thing to do is move on to another topic – one that you feel confident about – or have a bath, go for a walk, listen to music. Do anything for an hour or so that makes you feel better, but don't push yourself over the edge by staring blankly at your notes!

When you feel refreshed go over the topic again, but use a wildly different approach – copy a friend's revision notes, work through the problem backwards, break the topic unit into even smaller bits, or go back to basics by reading a text book or class notes.

Crush any negative feelings about the topic by finding somewhere new to study and by making out this is the first time you've revised it. Do whatever is necessary to wipe the slate clean so that your mind-set is positive.

Quit to win

> "I was hopeless at converting percentages to fractions, no matter what I tried. Always getting wrong answers made me feel so bad, I decided it was better to move on and make sure I earned top marks in all the other topics."
>
> Leigh (13)

After no end of effort in the final days before an exam, it is sometimes best to draw a line under a particular topic if it is eating away at your confidence and other exam preparation is suffering. Not a decision to be taken lightly and you have to be dead sure of your strengths in other topics.

It is not wise (and certainly not smart) to skip a topic or even part of a subject unit, gambling that it won't be in the paper.

Really good news

> "Isn't it too late to revise the day before the exam?"
>
> Calvin (14)

If you revise a topic that you have already studied and understood, your recall the next day after a good night's sleep will be at its peak. And with each revision, recall will be stronger and last longer. BUT anything learned for the first time the night before an exam (crammed, in other words) will not be reliably recalled the next day.

Solve

"I did okay in the mocks and my coursework is fine, but what if everything goes wrong on the day?"

Bobby (15)

Because you're warming up for your first exam, there's more on your mind than revision. No matter how well prepared, you're bound to have niggly worries about exam day. A three-day breathing space gives you plenty of time to work out what's worrying you AND time to find answers and solutions. The last thing you need the night before the exam is a tonne of 'What if's' keeping you awake – What if I'm late? What if I've forgotten a piece of equipment? What if I feel sick?

When a 'What if' question pops into your mind – it doesn't matter if it seems trivial or off-the-wall – write it down, and immediately find the answer.

Questions about how you might feel, act or behave in the exam can be talked through with a trusted friend (be careful, though, not to rattle a friend who is also sitting exams), family member or teacher. It doesn't matter how you arrive at the right answer for you, do it pronto so that a tiny worry doesn't grow into a mega one.

Here are solutions to some of the most frequently asked questions:

What if the paper is organised differently to last year?
Examiners are NOT into surprises or change for the sake of change, but if it has changed, your teachers will have been informed aeons ago and told you about it. Any changes will have been reflected in recent tests and mocks.

What if I take the wrong stuff into the exam?
You won't because you know what you need. Once you get to the exam location, teachers and friends will realise if you've forgotten something or are carrying an unauthorised bit of kit. For peace of mind, take extra pens and pencils, a spare battery for a calculator and some tissues.

What if nerves make me freeze up and go blank?
Forget 'freeze up and go blank' – neither will happen
because you know there are lots of ways to still those
butterflies in your stomach and to prompt information
that is on the tip of your tongue (see Chapter 7, page
104).

The moment you feel panic, get some perspective
by reminding yourself that a) it is just another exam,
b) you're ready for it and c) it will be over in less
time than it takes to watch a film.

If you feel yourself tensing up before or during the
test, you'll find some loosening up exercises under
Relax on page 120.

What if I'm late?
You won't be late because you know what time you
should arrive and you'll be ready to set off in good
time. Make sure your family knows your timetable so
that they can ring the alarm if you oversleep, give you
a lift and jolly you along (or totally ignore you if that
makes you feel better).

Should something beyond your control cause you to
be late or unable to attend (an accident en route, a
sudden illness, or serious personal or family crisis),
inform the school immediately and they will advise
you what to do and set the necessary procedures in
motion.

What if I've read the timetable wrong?
The short answer is – you won't. Friends, family and teachers just won't let something like that happen.

What if I'm running out of time in an exam?
The best advice is to go on and answer as many more questions as you can. Don't keep hammering at one question: no matter how much you write, the question has a maximum mark. Finish the question you are working on: an essay can be reduced to a properly worded introduction and conclusion with bullet-point notes for the middle, for example. For the remaining questions, work through them in order doing the ones you know the answers to and clearly marking those that require more thought. Go back and do the marked questions, possibly attempting the highest scoring ones first. Don't use your checking time to complete the paper: use it to check over what you have done.

What if everyone but me is really confident?
People react differently in times of stress. Some put on a really tough, confident show when they are jelly inside; others appear totally shaken when, in fact, they are keeping themselves very together. In short, appearances don't count for anything.

What you have to do is delete negative thinking. Instead, think 'You are going to do your best. You're going to thrash this paper.' In the days or hours before the test, avoid mixing with anyone who's into anxious chatter. Share a laugh and wish everyone luck, but keep focused on yourself.

What if I feel sick or want to go to the toilet?
If it's urgent, put your hand up and stand up at the same time, and move towards an invigilator. He or she will organise your safe and swift path to the loos.

If it's not so urgent, put up your hand to get an invigilator's attention. He or she will come to you. Invigilators certainly have an important job to do, but they are also human and will do their utmost to help.

Rehearse

"The teachers have told us what to expect, we've had mocks and lots of exam-condition tests, but I don't think they equal the real thing."

Shelley (14)

In the same way as going over past papers gives you confidence because you know what to expect, it can also help to rehearse or have a mental run-through of exam day, from getting ready at home through to finishing the paper. This is a positive bit of imagining, so everything builds towards the happy ending. Don't do this mental walk in real time – use the fast forward and only pause on the really good bits.

Imagine yourself on the morning of the exam prepared and ready, relaxed and confident. You wake-up bright and cheerful and arrive at school in good time. Your friends are there, so are one or two of your teachers. There's lots of well-wishing and silly jokes. You enter the exam room, look around to see all the familiar things and find your desk. You're feeling just great and can't wait for the exam to actually start. Lay out your equipment, get comfortable and check you can see the clock. You can see your best friends – they are smiling back at you. The invigilators seem very friendly, they are smiling and you can almost feel their encouragement. The instructions are clear and you've filled in the necessary details on the answer booklet. "You can start," says the invigilator. You read the instructions and look through the paper carefully. It all looks so familiar. You work well and there are no problems. Your timing is perfect, you complete every question and you've got five minutes to check over the paper. "Your time is up, please stop writing," says the invigilator. As the papers are collected, you know you've done your best.

You can rehearse anything you want: how you will answer certain sorts of questions, how you will retrieve information, how great you will feel when you answer a question on a difficult topic. Once you've imagined your exam it puts it in perspective and confirms that you are in control.

> **"You shouldn't build the exams into a big thing, but it's hard not to."**
>
> **Yas (16)**

TOP TIP

The day before an exam, gather all the things you will need – for example a calculator or an anthology if permitted. You will not be allowed to have a mobile phone – it's really important to remember that.

Relax

The day before an exam, set a cut-off time after which you will do no more revising. This curfew also means no quiet worrying or anxious pacing. Use the time to wind down and relax, and get things organised so that you go to bed ready to sleep.

"Don't stay up worrying the night before. Instead, think about how hard you have worked, how much you know and how you really deserve the rest."

Gail (15)

Before and during tests and exams use these methods to help you calm down and relax.

Take a breather

Place your hands on your lap so they are 'floppy' and let your shoulders and elbows drop. Close your eyes and concentrate on breathing slowly and deeply. Inhale through the nose, exhale through the mouth. Imagine yourself in a favourite place and relax your face muscles until you feel a smile forming. Keep the smile and get back to work. This routine can transform you in one minute.

Loosen up

- Spread your feet a little and place heels on the floor. Raise and lower feet and toes slowly five times to feel a stretch up the lower legs.
- Clench your buttocks five times to kill a 'numb bum'.
- Close your eyes and gently tilt your head to the left, back to the centre, and then to the right. Hold each position for a count of two and repeat the cycle two or three times. Keep your shoulders down and don't try to get your ear to touch your shoulder. This is a gentle stretch for neck and shoulder muscles.
- Let your arms drop to your sides loosely and roll your shoulders slowly forwards and backwards a couple of times.
- When your writing hand tires, put down your pen, let both arms dangle at your sides and wiggle your fingers to get the circulation going. While doing this you can read over an answer.
- For a big stretch, fake a yawn and stretch your arms up or out.

After each exam (if you don't have to go back to class) arrange to do something to take your mind off what you have just done and what is to come. Avoid milling around outside the exam room and dissecting the paper. That paper is history. It's done and dusted, finished, kaput – so forget about it!

> "The end of the exams was wonderful. I felt so free. I didn't even care what my results might be – I'd done my bit."
>
> Amy (16)

Contacts

Contact these authorities or visit their comprehensive websites for information on every aspect of your curriculum and tests and exams. Though some of the material is bureaucratic, there is valuable information and resources to be discovered.

Qualifications and Curriculum Authority (QCA)
Address: 83 Piccadilly, London W1J 8QA
Enquiries: 0207 509 5556
Web: www.qca.org.uk
(This site has links to the National Curriculum On-line and learning resources.)

Northern Ireland Council for Curriculum, Examinations and Assessments (CCEA)
Address: Clarendon Dock, 29 Clarendon Road, Belfast BT1 3BG
Enquiries: 02890 261 200   Web: www.ccea.org.uk

Scottish Qualifications Authority (SQA)
Glasgow office – The Optima Building, 58 Robertson Street, Glasgow G2 8DQ
Dalkeith office – Ironmills Road, Dalkeith, Midlothian EH22 1LE
Enquiries: 0845 279 1000   Web: www.sqa.org.uk
(Check out the on-line timetable builder to produce your own exam timetable and look at the National Grid for Learning's resource site, Scottish Virtual; Teachers' Centre – SVTC.)

Department for Education Lifelong Learning and Skills (DELLS), part of the Welsh Assembly
Address: Cathays Park, Cardiff, CF10 3NQ
Check website for regional offices.
Enquiries: 0845 010 3300   Web: www.learning.wales.gov.uk

Examination boards/groups

For information, sample papers, and examiner's expectations of GCSE exams, contact the relevant examining board. (Your school will tell you which exam boards/groups they are using for each subject.)

AQA   (consisting of AEB, SEG, NEAB) – Associated Examining Board, Southern Examination Group, Northern Examinations ans Assessment Board)
Web: www.aqa.org.uk
Check website for contact telephone numbers or phone your nearest office: Bristol: 0117 927 3437; Guildford 01483 596 506; Harrogate 01423 840 015; Manchester 0161 953 1180.

OCR/UCLES (consisting of MEG and OCEAC – Midlands Examining Group, Oxford and Cambridge Examinations and Assessment Council) – 01223 553 998   Web: www.ocr.org.uk

Edexcel Foundation 0870 240 9800
Web: www.edexcel.org.uk
Also check out the link on the Edexcel site to their excellent Examzone or go straight to www.examzone.co.uk

WJEC (Welsh Examination Council) – 029 2026 5000

Can't cope?

Both these advice and counselling services operate 24 hours a day, every day of the year. ChildLine 0800 1111
You can also contact them by mail: 45 Folgate Street, London, E1 6GL

Samaritans 08457 90 90 90 (UK) and 1850 60 90 90 (Rep of Ireland)
By post: Chris, PO Box 9090, Stirling, FK8 2SO
By email: jo@samaritans.org

The website addresses (URLs) included in this book were valid at the time of going to press. However, because of the nature of the Internet, it is possible that some addresses may have changed, or sites may have changed or closed down since publication. While the authors and Publishers regret any inconvenience this may cause the readers, no responsibility for any such changes can be accepted by either the author or the Publisher.

Index